The Now Zone

By Rick Manis

The Now Zone

By Rick Manis

Epmyrion Publishing

Winter Garden FL

info@EmpyrionPublishing.com

The Now Zone

Copyright © 2010 by Rick Manis

ISBN: 9781452835471

Empyrion Publishing
PO Box 784327
Winter Garden FL 34778
info@EmpyrionPublishing.com

Unless otherwise noted, all Scripture quotations are from the King James Version of the Bible.

Other versions are identified as the following:
NKJV-New King James Version
NIV- New International Version
BBE- The Bible in Basic English
NLT- New Living Translation
GWT- God's Word Translation
ISV- International Standard Version

Bold type is added by the author for emphasis.

Printed in the United States of America

Dedication

I dedicate this book to those who have faithfully held to God's promises, to those who have continued to believe, even while facing giants. You have stood on the Word of God. You have spoken His Word. At times you have cried out to God from your innermost being.

At times you felt like a failure, but you had nowhere to go except forward. There were times that you threw up your hands and thought you couldn't go on, but the Spirit pushed you, even when you tried to quit.

You are the reason I have written this book. I honor you and revere you. I know it's not always easy.

I thought of you on every page. You are a special kind of believer. You've been through much, but you are here going forward with God.

I believe that these followers of God are a chosen generation, and I believe that God is revealing a Word that will glorify these believers in a way that will draw creation to Him.

This is your time! I hope you enjoy the NOW ZONE.

Rick

Introduction

The Now Zone is a book I have been developing for over ten years. That's when the Lord introduced the revelation to me. Since then I have been learning it, living it, gaining biblical validation, and demonstrating it.

Early on, God began confirming this word to me with signs following. Personal prayers were being answered with miracles in a 24 hour period. When I started preaching it in churches, the same thing was happening to those who believed it.

I found out that if I could get people to believe me, absolutely anything could happen! There is such a joy in seeing those who have waited long for their prayers to be answered, and suddenly there it is!

I have received countless letters, emails, and phone calls with testimonies of miracle answers to prayer that came when they heard the message of *The Now Zone*. I hope you will let me know if something like that happens to you.

It is not my intention to make this revelation a new gadget or fad in Christianity. I really believe it is the most vital, missing element in our belief, and I believe it is something God is revealing in order to take His people to the top of the mountain.

It is with great joy and relief that I have completed this book. I have been faithful to the Father's command to preach the message in every church I have ministered to. He has been faithful to open the eyes of the hearers, and He has faithfully confirmed His Word, answering the cries of many hearts.

I have carried this message to my own circle of influence. Over the years it has been tried and tested. It has been refined and amplified by years of adding scripture to scripture, validating the concept of *The Now Zone* with the undeniable and rightly divided Word of God.

This book represents the "coming out" of my version of this message. I pray that more and more people will come to know this joyful sound!

Everyone hears the Word according to their own place of growth with God. To some of the readers of this book, the message will just make you go *"hmmm"*. For others, it will be a great source of inspiration.

For some of you however, it will be a whole new day! It will be like you have stepped into another world! I say this because it happened to me.

Welcome to *The Now Zone* which is simply the realm of God. It's a place where time is not a buffer or barrier between you and your blessings.

ENJOY!

Contents

Chapter 1

Waiting on God's Timing?

I was walking that familiar mile to the post office. I had to. I was going to check the post box to see if someone had sent money to support our ministry. It was a gorgeous day for a walk, but I would've rather been driving.

Teresa and I were without wheels. We had no ride. Our car had been recently totaled by a hit and run driver who rear ended it while Teresa was driving. It was a decent, dependable car in nice shape. It was also paid for, so we only carried the required liability insurance. Without full coverage, no culpable driver, and absolutely no money, we had no way of obtaining another automobile.

Our financial struggles had led us to a condition where our credit was maxed out, damaged, and cut off. Even if we could have borrowed more, we couldn't have made any payments. We were fighting with all of our might just to pay the obligations at hand.

We did, however, believe that God would provide. He had done miracles for us before. We knew He could, and would, do it again. So we prayed, asked, and spoke that God had a car for us. We had no idea how He would pull this off, but it would be fun to watch Him do it.

That was our attitude. We were upbeat, positive, and full of faith. What else could we do? We were against the wall, and The Lord was our only source.

This wasn't exactly new to us. We had been in similar situations many times. Somehow, we always made it through. It seemed that we lived a lot with our back against a wall. It also seemed that God would do His thing at the last possible moment, late in the midnight hour so to speak. Actually, we had become quite accustomed to hanging on to the end of a rope, and being rescued by God at the last minute. This had become a pattern.

As the days without a car passed, it became harder to be excited about the pending miracle. It really wasn't fun. To get around, we borrowed cars, rented cars, rode with friends, rode the metro bus, and walked.

You Can Have It Whenever You're Ready

As I walked to the post office that day, I was praising and thanking God for my upcoming car miracle. Thinking about it, I realized it had now been a couple of weeks since the rear end collision. I didn't know why God had not done it yet, but I was sure it was a timing thing. He had His reasons, and He would do it in His time, which was perfect. So I assured Him that I understood, and that I would be happy to continue waiting, if that's what He wanted.

Then the Holy Spirit interrupted my prayer. I clearly heard Him say, "You can have that car whenever you're ready. Your car is within you."

My immediate reply was, "I've been ready for two weeks!"

The Lord answered, "No, you've been *needy* for two weeks, but you haven't been *ready*".

I had the green light from God! I wasn't waiting on Him, *He was waiting on me.* My ideas about God's timing had me settling for nothing every day for two weeks. How could I really have faith while thinking it may not be God's will to give it to me yet? I needed to stir up my faith. I needed to get to that powerful place of expectation. I needed to find within me, the faith that creates miracles. My car was within me!

"But ye, beloved, building up yourselves on your most holy faith, praying in the Holy Ghost" – Jude 1:20

When I got home, I went into prayer, determined to "pray through". I needed to pray until I had a conviction. I needed to pray until there was no doubt. I needed to pray until I knew that I knew that I knew!

Finally, I was there. I felt strong, bold, and expectant. I would have to wait no more! My car was within me, and I would bring it into the physical realm. *It was my call.* My heavenly Father said so.

I was departing on a ministry trip the next morning. I told Teresa to change my airline ticket to "one way". I would be driving a car back. God had a miracle for me, and I was *ready*!

I preached the first of three nightly meetings, and the next day I got together with a good friend who lives in the area. He asked what I wanted to do that day.

My answer was, "Take me to a car dealer. I'm going to pick out a car".

We went. I chose the one I wanted, and told the salesman I would be back tomorrow to pay for it.

That night after the service, I was approached in the church parking lot by a lady who had been in the services both nights. She introduced me to her husband, who wanted to talk with me. I had never met him before. He told me that he meant to be in that night's service, but got busy and couldn't get away. He also said that God spoke to him that afternoon, saying that I needed a lot of money "for something big like, a house or car or something", as he put it.

"Is that true?" he asked.

I said, "Yes it is".

I had not told *anyone*, nor did I mention it in the church service. In fact, it didn't enter my mind until I was confronted by this stranger. No one else knew except my friend, and he wasn't in attendance that night.

I told the man about the car I picked out, and how I was trusting God for a miracle.

He asked me how much I needed. I told him the exact price of the car.

He then wrote out a check for the full amount.

What if?

What if I had continued to hold onto my former beliefs about God's timing? What if The Lord had not corrected me with a *now* word? Would I have prayed with the same expectation?

What if I had not decreed and committed to having my prayer met immediately? Would that man have written me a check? Notice that God spoke to him that afternoon, *after* I told the salesman that I would be back to pay for the car. If I'm not buying a car that day, I don't need that check.

I realized at that time that we could hasten the "showing up" of The Lord. I realized that a lot of times we think we are waiting on God, when He is really waiting on *us*. I realized that there is a place in God where *waiting* is short circuited, where *time* is not a buffer between me and my blessing. I realized that God does not live in time as we know it, and we can live in *His* realm!

The Lord had spoken to me. He had confirmed His Word with signs following. I had found a new level, a new place to walk. Anything could happen! This was the place of miracles - now!

In the days that followed I received a mandate from God. It was a command to preach a message to everyone He sent me to. I was to know this message, explain it, make it plain, convince people, and demonstrate it.

The Lord told me, "I want you to get my people into THE NOW ZONE".

Chapter 2

Ten Years Becomes One Hour

It seemed that everything I saw in the Bible was saying "Now". I felt I was soon able to preach and teach it with conviction and solid scripture.

The first time I ever preached "The Now Zone", I declared to the congregation that God was going to take time out of their struggle. I remember preaching from John 2:19, where Jesus said He could raise up a temple in three days.

Those who heard Him said it was impossible, for it had taken men 46 years to build the temple.

I suddenly received prophetic inspiration and stated with authority, "The Lord is saying that what normally takes over 40 years of labor, He will do in three days! What normally takes 20 years of Christian progress He will do in *one day*! What has in the past taken 10 years of spiritual labor, God will do in *one hour*!"

I continued to speak as the Lord gave me utterance, "For instance", I said, "Some of you may have labored, prayed, and stood in faith for the salvation of a loved one. It may have seemed like the more you prayed, the meaner they became. You've fought discouragement, but you have determined to keep on trusting for as long as it takes. God says He will now do that work *in one hour*!"

I preached on and on, spouting scriptures. Afterwards, a line of people came forward for prayer, mostly for healing. It was good. People were being instantly healed. About halfway through the line, I came to a lady whose face was soaked with tears. I asked her what she wanted.

She proceeded to tell me that I had described her in my message that night. Her husband was not interested in living for the Lord. She had prayed for his salvation for years with no result. The spiritual labor had been long and hard.

I felt so sorry for her. I began to do the only thing I knew. I quoted God's promise that, if we would believe, we would be saved *along with all of our house*. I prayed the prayer of agreement, quoting that if we would agree, it would be done.

Then something happened. An awesome boldness got all over me. I looked the lady in the eye and said, "Sister, right now that man of yours is calling on the Lord. He's becoming a new creation right now. When you get home tonight, you will find a new husband!"

She began to laugh and rejoice. The church went wild with praise and rejoicing. The louder they got, the bigger I felt! I felt strong, anointed, and full of faith and power!

I reveled in this feeling for about sixty seconds. Then my emotions quickly changed.

As I proceeded down the prayer line, God was still moving. People were being healed. Everything continued to look awesome as I ministered to the folks, but in my mind a conflict had begun.

I scolded myself, "Rick, who do you think you are? All you had to do was stand on the scripture and agree in prayer.

That's all you needed to do, but no. That wasn't spectacular enough. You had to show off. You had to go out on a limb. You've gotten her hopes up. What if she goes home and her husband is still the same? She will be more discouraged than ever before. You will be a false prophet. The word will get out, and you will be out of business".

These were my actual thoughts as I continued to pray for the people. Nobody noticed. Outwardly I was blessing the people. Inwardly, there was an argument.

However, even the negative thoughts didn't last long. The service was so good that I became overwhelmed with the satisfaction of being in a wonderful service. The preaching had come in power. God's presence was strong and the people were very happy and blessed. It really was a great night. The negative thoughts had come and gone, and I forgot all about it... ...until a few days later.

"Rick, do you remember?"

The pastor's wife called a week after the meeting to let me know how they appreciated it, and how the people were blessed by it. It gave me a sense of fulfillment to hear her tell of the praise reports from that service.

Then her voice turned solemn as she posed a question, "Rick, uh, do you remember telling a lady that her husband would be saved that night?"

I had forgotten all about that. There were so many good things to remember about the meeting. It never crossed my mind once after that, but there it was in my face. I remembered. I felt a little nervous. What was the pastor's wife about to say?

I swallowed, then replied "Oh yeah, I remember that". My mind began trying to think of ways to explain why it may not have happened.

She told me that the lady's husband wanted to stay home and watch TV that night rather than go to church, but he turned to the wrong channel. A televangelist caught his attention. The minister was praying on the air, calling out healings with the word of knowledge. He specifically spoke the name of the husband, saying it was time for him to give his heart to the Lord. The man prayed for salvation right then and there! He was born again!

You can imagine how happy I was to hear that, and how happy the lady was to meet her new man when she got home that night!

What a glorious sight it was the next time I went to that church. I looked out at the congregation during the singing.

There they were with tears, holding hands upraised to the Father in worship.

The Lord had confirmed His Word with signs following.

"There you go again."

I shared that story with the next church I preached in. It was a Sunday morning and the crowd received the message with fervor. It was a revival atmosphere with people jumping up out of their seats, waving and shouting.

I was scheduled to speak in both the morning and evening service. I don't remember what I preached that night, but afterward, while praying for those who came forward, I came to a lady with a green shirt folded in her hands.

When I asked about the shirt, she told me that she was in the same situation that the lady in my story had been in. She also had been praying long for her husband's salvation. She said that the shirt in her hands was his favorite, and he wore it "all the time".

I laid my hands on it and declared it as our point of contact. I quoted the promise of her household salvation. I prayed the prayer of agreement that this desire of her heart would be done.

Then something happened.

That awesome boldness got all over me again. I looked the lady in the eye and said, "Sister, the next time your husband puts this shirt on, the anointing of God will get all over him. He will bow his knee and make Jesus his lord and savior!"

She began to laugh and rejoice. The church went wild with praise and rejoicing. The louder they got, the bigger I felt! I felt strong, anointed, and full of faith and power!

I reveled in this feeling for about sixty seconds. Then my emotions quickly changed.

As I proceeded down the prayer line, God was still moving. People were being healed. Everything continued to look awesome as I ministered to the folks, but in my mind a conflict had begun ...again.

I scolded myself, "Rick, there you go again. God bailed you out when you tried this before, but you can't arbitrarily spout out anything and think that God will do your bidding. Thou shalt not tempt the Lord thy God."

(Satan is a whisperer, our adversary. We find the voice of the enemy in our own thoughts, imaginations, and arguments against the knowledge of God. This voice is only heard when our thinking has not been conformed to the ways of the only true God.)

Again, those negative thoughts did not last long. I was too involved in the service, which was glorious. God continued to bless the people that night. I was very happy with the meeting, and forgot all about the green shirt... ...until Wednesday.

"Hey Preacher, do you remember?!"

At the end of that Sunday night service, the pastor asked if I could come back Wednesday and preach through Saturday. It just so happened that I was to minister at another church in the area on Sunday, and had nothing scheduled in between. So it worked perfectly.

When I arrived at the Wednesday service, the worship was already in progress and the house was full. I made my way to the front row and sat on the end, near the wall. I sat with my head bowed, listening for God's direction. I wasn't paying much attention to things going on around me. After the singing, I heard people testifying, but I just continued to sit and commune with the Lord. Then a voice in the crowd caught my ear.

"Hey Preacher!" the voice called.

I turned my head and saw that the only person in the congregation who was standing was a lady looking straight at me from the farthest corner in the back. I waved at her, and she pointed at me as she continued to speak.

"Do you remember that shirt you prayed for the other night?" she said, thrusting her finger toward me.

I had forgotten all about it, but now it came back to confront me. What was she about to say? She looked intense. I couldn't tell by her face if she was angry or excited.

I answered "Oh… yeah."

"Well here it is!" She pointed down at the man sitting next to her in the green shirt. He was crying into his hands and shaking uncontrollably. The anointing was all over him!

The church shouted and praised God. The man walked that long aisle to make a public confession of Jesus Christ as his Lord and savior.

The Lord had confirmed His Word with signs following.

Since then, I have seen countless times when God brought the waiting of His people to an end. It's like they were following a carrot on a stick, and they finally grabbed it!

If a promise from God seems like it's always ahead of you, but not yet in your hands, then this book will be good news! You are about to lose the buffer and barrier to the manifestation of your promise! Your enemy is called "time". It has made you wait for something that's already been done for you.

As you continue in this book, fresh vision, faith and expectation will arise! The Holy Spirit will walk you out of the tyranny of time, and into THE NOW ZONE.

It Will Happen!

I have heard for decades that we are the generation that would walk in God's glory like no other generation has. I have heard prophecies of a healing anointing that would clean out hospitals. I believe these things.

I also believe that you and I have personal vision, a sense of destiny, and a knowing of some things that God has promised for our lives individually. Some of these things are so awesome that only God could initiate such vision, but we really believe that these things are in God's plan for us.

However, the vision and the promises are so big that God will have to speed things up, because at the rate it's been going, we wouldn't make it. We can't keep waiting for even the smallest of these things.

I have good news! God has promised to speed things up. You are about to see an acceleration in your life!

Let me show you some prophecies that promise a day when we would not have to wait on God any more…

Chapter 3

A New Pattern

"...what is this proverb that you people have... which says, „The days are prolonged, and every vision fails? Tell them therefore, „Thus says the Lord GOD: "I will lay this proverb to rest, and they shall no more use it as a proverb in Israel." But say to them, "The days are at hand, and the fulfillment of every vision... and the word which I speak will come to pass; it will no more be postponed; for in your days... I will say the word and perform it," says the Lord GOD."

Again the word of the LORD came to me, saying, "Son of man, look, the house of Israel is saying, „The vision that he sees is

for many days from now, and he prophesies of times far off."
Therefore say to them, „Thus says the Lord GOD: "None of
My words will be postponed any more..." – Ezekiel 12:21-26
NKJV

Our past experience has taught us that God's Word and
vision takes a long time. It has become our expectation, but
God can change that pattern! He promises to change our
doctrine. We see in the above verse, a prophetic declaration of
a day of every vision being fulfilled! We see that the Word
would no longer be postponed! We see that the speaking and
the happening of the Word would come together at the same
time!

"Behold, the days come, saith the LORD, that the plowman
shall overtake the reaper, and the treader of grapes him that
soweth seed..." – Amos 9:13

This verse is a mouthful, but it essentially means that
by the time you've thrown the seed in the ground, the harvest is
coming up in your face! By the time you've spoken the Word,
the manifestation in your hands. The reaping and sowing
become the same season!

This is a marvelous concept, but God promised that
those days would come! So they have to come. Could it be

now? Is God revealing such things to us in order to bring that day into our lives?

This prophecy is the promise of a new pattern to live by! In the past, our pattern was seed, then time (or waiting), then harvest. Time, or waiting, was usually a very long season. You probably have had some seeds in the ground for years, and you're still waiting; but what if God took time out of the equation? You would have a new pattern of seed and harvest. You would actually be living like a son of God, like Jesus who spoke and it happened! People marveled that a man could speak and it would actually happen.

We are destined to be conformed to that image (Romans 8:29), but we must adopt a new pattern. We need a new mindset and belief system. God's Word will transform us by the renewing of our minds.

"And it shall come to pass, that before they call, I will answer; and while they are yet speaking, I will hear". – Isaiah 65:24

Here is a promise of the quick answers to prayer. I know we are in the day that Isaiah was speaking of. There have been times when my wife and I would pray for something, and that very day or the next it would arrive in a package at our door. Someone had sent it *before we asked*!

How's that for taking the wait out of our walk?!

"And he swore by him who lives forever and ever, who created the heavens and all that is in them, the earth and all that is in it, and the sea and all that is in it, and said, "There will be no more delay!" – Rev. 10:6 NIV

"And if the Lord had not made the time short, no flesh would have been kept from destruction; but because of the saints he has made the time short." – Mark 13:20 BBE

If God does not change this issue of time and waiting, we won't get it! We will die without seeing our full destiny. Our healing won't come fast enough. The Lord knows this, so because of us He has promised to speed things up.

Most Christians spend their life climbing a spiritual mountain, trying to arrive at the high calling of God in Christ. Most of them die somewhere on the side of that mountain. They made great progress, but they were always on a journey.

What would be wrong with a generation of believers who are *standing* on top of the mountain? Then they could live their lives in fullness! They could bless creation like sons of God should! That sounds more like the will of God to me.

"But you have come to Mount Zion, to the heavenly Jerusalem, the city of the living God. You have come to thousands upon thousands of angels in joyful assembly." – Heb. 12:22 NIV

Is that alright with you? Can you receive a life of no more waiting for things that are already provided in our covenant with God? Would it be okay if you spoke and it happened? Shouldn't it be normal for us to live and operate like Jesus, since we are also sons of God?

Get ready for a new normal! You have this book because things are about to change!

But first, we have to get rid of some false ideas about the timing of God...

Chapter 4

What's This Tarrying Business?

I used to always hear about a "tarrying" God. We would gather for church next Sunday, "If the Lord tarries".

I pictured a tarrying God who was somewhat impervious to our suffering. We would cry out for help, and the Lord would tarry. He had not rescued us from the earth yet for only one reason. He was tarrying.

Preachers would say that they could just imagine Jesus standing up, ready to come and get us; but the Father wouldn't give the green light. He was tarrying. His reply: "Not yet. Let them wait".

To me, this was what God did best – tarry. It often seemed that it was *all* God did. He *always* tarried.

People on earth were scrambling and praying. They needed healing, financial miracles, homes restored, peace of mind. They fasted. They cried out from their innermost being. They praised. They worshipped. They sowed a financial seed…

…and God tarried.

I really don't find this "tarrying" business in the Word of God. I think the church made that up to try to explain why we didn't get answers to our prayers. Oh, what damage is done by preaching a tarrying God!

I was taught about a slow God. He always showed up late in the midnight hour. We sang about it. We expected it. We lived it.

"…according to your faith be it unto you." – Matthew 9:29

Our faith said that we had a God who liked to wait until we couldn't stand it anymore. He would watch us squirm and struggle and try to hold on until we slipped to the end of our rope.

We never even expected Him to do a quick work, our God was, *"Slow, but never too late".*

Did you ever hear that line?

My faith became accustomed to that kind of God. No matter how hard I prayed and try to receive by faith, somehow I *knew* that there would be a period of time before my answer actually came.

This was my image of God. Did you hear that? I had made an *image* of God. In my own mind was an *image* made of earthly materials (doctrines).

It is no wonder that God doesn't want us to make an image of Him. It will always be less than who He really is, and the image left me suffering all too often.

God is light! That's fast!

Before you had a need, God provided the answer through Jesus. That's fast!

*"...His throne was like the fiery flame, and **His wheels as burning fire."** –* Daniel 7:9

That's fast! God doesn't wear a watch. He is not bound by time, and He is bringing you into His realm.

He's taking time out of your struggle…

Chapter 5

Losing the Wait

In John chapter two, Jesus attended a marriage. When the wine had run out, His mother came to Him, obviously wanting Him to do something about it.

His answer to her was, "Woman what have I to do with thee? Mine hour is not yet come" (John 2:4).

In essence, Jesus was saying that it was not time for Him to come out publicly. *It wasn't time* to do miracles. Think about it. The Lord Himself denied Mary's request based not on lack of ability or need, but on *timing*.

However, Mary acted as though Jesus would do it anyway, telling the servants to follow His orders. Apparently, she didn't take "no" for an answer.

Guess what? Jesus made wine! Think about *that*. The Lord Himself declared that the timing was all wrong. What would you do if you asked the Lord for something and He simply said it wasn't time yet? You would probably do what most would do, which is to just say "ok", right? What other options are there? You got your answer: "wait", "later", "not now".

But what if you persisted on receiving it now? What if you didn't take "wait" for an answer? Would the Lord be displeased?

Notice that Jesus, who declared that it was NOT time for such things, made it time anyway! Mary expected wine that day, not later. The wedding is today, not tomorrow. Next week won't do. We need wine today!

The Lord always loves a heart that expects to receive. I can find no example in scripture where He became angry or disgusted by someone who insisted on now manifestations. In fact, I only find Him being bothered by a lack of expectancy.

Another Example

In Matthew chapter fifteen, a Syrian woman implores Jesus to come and heal her daughter who was demon possessed. Again, Jesus turns someone down because of timing. He tells her that it wouldn't be right to "take the children's bread and throw it to the dogs", since He was only sent to the house of Israel.

Was Jesus racist? We He cold hearted? Was it God's will that she not be helped?

NO!

The only issue was timing. Jesus knew what His earthly calling was. He was sent by the Father to minister for three years to Israelites, but if the Syrian woman can just wait, she can eventually be helped. After the Lord's resurrection, He would empower His apostles and send them to the gentiles. Then all of the other people of the world could have what Jesus was giving to the Israelites.

So it was just a matter of time. If she can just stand the torment for a while, help will come from the Lord by and by. If she will just be patient, it will all be better someday.

But she still believed that she could have it now anyway. She persisted, and it really, really pleased the Lord!

"But without faith it is impossible to please Him: for he that cometh to God must believe that he is, and that he is a rewarder of them that diligently seek him." – Heb. 11:6

Jesus got excited about her faith and gave her what she wanted. When it wasn't time, He made it time!

According To Your Faith...

I remember a church service, where I was praying for the sick with a very strong anointing. It was so smooth and marvelous. People were getting instant and full manifestations of healing, and I could feel the power of God touching them.

But there was one particular elderly lady who had a strong spiritual presence. You could feel that she was a woman who was serious about God. She had probably known the Lord for quite some time, and was obviously a woman of great prayer.

With the help of her cane, she made her way to the front for prayer. God was moving, and His power was all over me. With confidence, I approached her to pray for her, and as soon as I touched her... the anointing was gone!

This was strange. I prayed two or three times, feeling and seeing no evidence of healing. She walked back to her seat, the only person who left the same as they came.

After the meeting was dismissed, I stood near the platform visiting with people. The elderly lady came to me and thanked me for praying for her.

Then, with the confidence of one who was older, more experienced, and more knowledgeable than I, she began to "teach" me that God will only heal her when He decides that it is time.

I knew then exactly why the anointing left when I touched her. She had rejected the "now" message and her belief about God's timing kept her from receiving her healing.

There are so many people who love the Lord. They pray. They live right. They love and they give, yet they wait and do without the blessings of God. It's not because they lack zeal, or good deeds, or obedience. It's because of a lack of knowledge.

"My people are destroyed for lack of knowledge..." – Hosea 4:6

It's *always* a lack of knowledge, nothing else. We have lacked knowledge of God, but the life of Jesus reveals the true way of God. Jesus lived, demonstrated, and taught a "now" kingdom, or NOW ZONE.

And His death and resurrection would bring man back to the "now" life…

Chapter 6

Jesus Restores the Now

Jesus stood up to read in the synagogue and was handed the book of Isaiah. He scanned the scrolls and found what He was looking for, God's promise of restoration. He read of a day when the brokenhearted would be healed, the captives would be free, the blind would see. There would be no more oppression, for it would be a perpetual jubilee.

Those in attendance were familiar with these promises. Such promises of the future were often repeated among the believing. I can imagine that their responses were something equivalent to our modern church responses of "preach it", "come on", "glory", "well", "amen", "up in here!" Their hearts were stirred as they were reminded of a soon coming day.

Their eyes were fixed on Jesus as they waited for His comment on the scripture reading. He sat down and announced, "Today, this scripture is fulfilled in your hearing" (Luke 4:21).

Suddenly, the atmosphere began to change. Confusion rolled across the room, then anger. The church people thrust Jesus out of the city, and tried to throw their Messiah off of a cliff.

They knew that this could not be the One, and this was surely not the day they were waiting for.

Religion Never Says "Now"

The people could not accept the fact that the day of promises fulfilled was that very day. Those who follow religion are not in shape to receive.

Religion is great about making promises, but is awful when it comes to receiving the promises. Religion will speak wonderful things about God, but it will never let you have it now. Religion is a cruel master that seems to hate the idea of having God's fullness now. Even as you read this book, you will notice religion trying all it can to put your fullness off into the future.

But Jesus came to give *good news*! He commanded us to preach *good news*! What was the good news?

"And as ye go, preach, saying, The kingdom of heaven is at hand." – Matthew 10:7

The realm of Heaven is near! It's so near that now we can reach out and partake! Everywhere Jesus went, He demonstrated the realm of Heaven. Nobody had to wait. They were healed, forgiven, restored. The scripture Jesus read from Isaiah was literally happening!

Jesus introduced the message that all things are possible with God. There would be no more limitations or restraints! The day mankind has cried out for has come. It was restored by the Son of God.

"For all of God's promises have been fulfilled in Christ with a resounding „Yes!"" – II Cor. 1:20 NLT

Wow! Look at all of the promises made in the Bible. They are no longer a future event. They have been fulfilled! You don't need to just have a great future. You have a great present!

"Blessed be the God and Father of our Lord Jesus Christ, who hath blessed us with all spiritual blessings in heavenly places in Christ." – Ephesians 1:3

What are we waiting for? Is it another dispensation, another move of God? Why is everything "later"? God has given us ALL THINGS through Christ, past tense!

"His divine power has given us everything we need for life and godliness..." – II Pet. 1:3 NIV

If You Can Receive It

The disciples once asked Jesus if Elijah would come (Matthew 17:10).

His answer was that Elijah will come and restore all things, but also that Elijah had already come in John the Baptist.

"And if you are willing to accept it, he is the Elijah who was to come." – Matt. 11:14

Are we still looking for the spirit and power of Elijah that Malachi, the scribes, and Jesus said would come and bring restoration? Or did it already come? It depends on you.

You can look forward to a day of restoration, or you can accept, and benefit from, a restoration that is already here!

Your perception determines your reality. You can only partake of a "now" benefit if you are willing to receive it as *now*.

I can prophecy that God is going to heal you. It might give you a lot of hope and expectation, but *if you can receive it*, by His stripes you WERE healed!

I can pray that God will bless you, but *if you can receive it,* He has already blessed you with every blessing in Christ Jesus! If you are blessed, you won't wish for blessing. If you are blessed, you feel and act blessed. You have a confidence in your blessed status, making it easy to receive all of God's goodness.

This is THE NOW ZONE. It is a knowing that God is not holding out or saving the good stuff for later. When you know that, receiving becomes automatic. The struggle is over, and you experience the will of God, which is "on earth as it is in Heaven" (Matthew 18:19).

"...the LORD will give grace and glory: no good thing will He withhold from them that walk uprightly." – Psalm 84:11

To walk uprightly is to walk like a son of God. Don't slouch. Walk uprightly. Lift up your head and walk like someone who has been blessed with all things that pertain to life and Godliness. When you do, you find blessings overtaking you.

Welcome to the kingdom of Heaven! It's a realm, or reality that transcends time and space. It's supernatural. It's God's world and He isn't bound by time. His nature is NOW. His name is "Now"…

Chapter 7

God's Name is "Now"

When God sent Moses to free the Israelites from Egypt, Moses said, "What if they ask me your name? What will I tell them?"

The Lord's reply was, "I am who I am. Tell them *I Am* has sent you".

"I am" is a present form of the verb "to be". It is not "I was", or "I will be". It is a word that always points to NOW.

It is this word, "I am" that is the root of God's name *Yahweh* or *Jehovah*, which means "God existent", or "God that is". The point is very clear. His name means NOW!

"And I appeared unto Abraham, unto Isaac, and unto Jacob, by the name of God Almighty, but by my name JEHOVAH was I not known to them." – Exodus 6:3

The Israelites knew God as the God of the patriarchs, and the God of the promise. They knew Him as the God who once did, and would do again; but they did NOT know Him by His name, Jehovah, or I Am, (or NOW).

Why did God send Moses with a name that the Israelites did not know? Because they needed to know God in a new and living way! God had to become the God of NOW, not yesterday, or some day. For over 400 years the Israelites held to a promise of the future, but it was never a promise of NOW.

According to your faith be it unto you. If it's going to get better tomorrow, tomorrow never comes. Every day that you wake up, tomorrow is just a day out of reach.

*"...God is our refuge and strength, an ever-**present** help in trouble."* – Psalm 46:1 NIV

The *promise* has to become the *present*. *Tomorrow's* God has to become *today's* God! He doesn't live in the future.

He lives in the NOW. It's people that put everything off into the future.

We need to be spiritually aware. Truth makes us free. God is calling man into His realm. It's the upward calling of God in Christ. It's the "Come up hither" cry of Heaven. Since His ways and thoughts are not ours, He calls us to forsake our ways so we can live in His way (the now zone).

"Let the wicked forsake his way, and the unrighteous man his thoughts...

For my thoughts are not your thoughts, neither are your ways my ways, saith the LORD." – Isaiah 55:7-8

The Lure and Hype of "About To"

"God is about to do something..."

"There's a mighty outpouring coming..."

"A move of God is just around the corner..."

We (the church) have preached and prophesied these words over and over for years. We stir giant congregations in conventions with an exciting call to get ready for what God's about to do.

It seems that God is always *preparing* to do something. We are always preaching about later.

That message inspires the church. It gives them a reason to keep going, though they are tired and have waited long. It justifies our present suffering.

With that message we can feel special again. We relate to the Bible characters who spent long years in tribulation, and were blessed abundantly later.

There is great truth to that message! And I use it often to encourage folks who find it hard to see through their trouble. Everyone needs to at least have hope in God!

But there is a more powerful message. It speaks on a higher level, and many people who have been living on a hope that's "just around the corner" can *turn* the corner if they hear the NOW Word!

Hope is a promise. Faith is NOW. If we can see the truth that makes us free, we no longer have to live like Old Testament men. Jesus has come! Things are different! He suffered for us! He paid for the crime, and *He did the time*!

Did you ever notice that the word "faith" is only found three times in the Old Testament? In one place it said the people had no faith. The other statement, spoken twice, promised that the just would live by faith.

Then in the New Testament the word is used countless times, on nearly every page! It's a new and living way! All things are now possible! The work has been done for us!

Hope is where wilderness wanderers spend their time. They are very needy, but have strength to continue because of a promised land. Hope is good. Without it we all would have quit a long time ago, but hope is not home, no more than the wilderness was home for the Israelites.

One of the problems with hope is that if you live in it long enough, it *feels* like home. It becomes your reality. You get so used to it, that you cannot leave!

When the Israelites were first led to the door of their promised land, they rejected their opportunity to move into it.

"When your fathers tempted me, proved me, and saw my works forty years. Wherefore I was grieved with that generation, and said, They do always err in their heart; and they have not known my ways." – Heb. 3:9-10

If they had learned His *ways*, they would have possessed their promised land. They saw many miracles, and those miracles sustained them, but inwardly, they never took on the nature, attitude, and way of the Lord. If they had learned to see things the way God does, they would have responded in faith.

They looked at the inhabitants of Canaan. The inhabitants were larger and more numerous, and they had strong fortresses. The Israelites simply could not accept victory yet. In their eyes, they just weren't there yet. They needed to "grow". They were still small. They didn't have the numbers. Maybe later, when they became glorious shiny powerhouses it could happen.

God was ready. They weren't. God had prepared everything, but they couldn't get out of the mindset of "later".

It's strange that we can want deliverance so bad, yet our mindset won't let it happen. When your mind is stuck in hope, it's hard to shift into NOW faith.

It takes a new sound to transform us by renewing our mind to the NOW world of God. It takes a fresh Word to cause new things to spring forth! Do you dare to turn and look at a finished work of Christ?

The walk you're coming into is *not* a replication of some Old Testament, unregenerate man. This is a new and living way! It's the way of the Lord.

Are you ready to break the pattern of the past?

Read on…

Chapter 8

Breaking the Paradigm of the Past

You cannot judge your tomorrow by your yesterday. To do so is to be stuck in a rut. A rut is formed by frequent travel in the same path. Then it seems to be the *only* path, and it's hard to go any other direction.

This happens in our mindset. Without trying, we expect certain things to be according to a pattern ingrained in us. God wants to break the pattern! Your tomorrow is NOT your today. Your alpha is not your omega.

But we have to buy into a new season, a new song, and new things springing forth. They don't happen until our belief system is renewed to the NOW existence.

In Luke chapter five, Peter had come in from fishing all night with no luck. Jesus told him to launch into the deep and cast his *nets* for a big catch.

Peter complained that he had already been there and done that, and done it to no avail, but he would obey anyway and cast out the *NET*. I emphasize that Jesus said *nets* (plural), and Peter only cast a *net* (singular).

Jesus did not ask how hard it was the night before. He did not ask how long the disciple had labored. Jesus did not ask about Peter's lack of success. It was a new day! Today had nothing to do with last night. So what if it was a certain way last night. What does that have to do with now? That was then. This is NOW!

Peter expected the same results as he had before. That's why he grudgingly threw out only one net. Surprise! He quickly found out that he wasn't prepared for what the Lord had prepared for him!

His net began to break. His boat nearly capsized. Jesus had broken the pattern.

God has prepared everything you need for life and Godliness. The question is, are YOU prepared to receive it? I hope you are joyfully taking on a new season mentality. As a man thinketh in his heart, so is he. If you think you can have it NOW, you're right! If you think you must keep waiting, you're right.

You're belief will automatically produce outward manifestations. Instead of looking around and waiting to see if things are changing in the world around you, get excited about changing you!

You have to know that the same belief in "later" will only keep your manifestations in the future.

NOW are we the sons of God, with a NOW faith in a NOW God, living in the kingdom NOW!

In John chapter two, Jesus told the Pharisees that if they would tear the temple down, He would raise it up in three days.

Their response was, "No way!" They said it took 46 years to build the temple.

Again, Jesus didn't care how long things used to take. He didn't care how hard it was before. Jesus would do a new thing. He would break the pattern of the past!

In II Kings chapter seven, there was a famine in the city of Samaria. It was so severe that the people were eating donkey head and dove's dung. Some began eating their children. It was bad!

The king called for Elisha the prophet, who said that tomorrow at the same time, there would be abundance and everyone would have it.

The king's assistant said, "No way! Even if God brings rain it will take time to raise a crop".

Elisha said, "Snooze you lose. Everyone except you will have it."

The normal pattern had to be broken. While seedtime and harvest will always be as long as the earth remains, God has SUPERNATURAL ways that transcend the normal pattern!

God sent some hungry lepers to the enemy's camp. As they went, the Lord scared the enemy with the sound of an army. The lepers found an abandoned camp with food, clothing, gold and silver. They took it back to the city and everyone (except the king's assistant, who was trampled in the rush) had abundance. They didn't have to wait on the old time table. God has ways of speeding things up!

He broke the pattern of the past. Anything can happen in the NOW ZONE!

The pattern of seedtime and harvest is always available. It's good and it works for saint and sinner alike; but what really excites me is this *new and living way*!

Stuck in "Wait" Mode

When you've been in a pattern for a long time, it becomes like home. It becomes a part of your identity. Your mind becomes hard-wired so that it becomes your "normal" existence.

When we've been waiting for something for a long time, we become more accustomed to *waiting* than *receiving*. After a while, we get stuck in "wait" mode. Every day that we wake up, we automatically expect to continue waiting. This is a pattern that is not easily broken!

That's when you need a NEW sound that is sent to break the old sound barrier, a certain sound from Heaven! That sound is the sound of NOW! It has the power to bring you into the fullness of God if you can hear it!

A new sound offers a new door of opportunity. Before you lies a different way. Do you dare to enter a place of promises fulfilled, a place of rest, and a place that few have found? Do you dare to lose every reason to wait? Are you willing to let your old belief system crumble?

If so read on, and get ready for some high speed, high definition, up to date, cutting edge, *spiritechnology*!

Those who heard the Good News in the past did not enter God's place of rest...So God set another day. That day is today...God spoke about it through David..."If you hear God speak today, don't be stubborn." – Heb. 4:6-7 GWT

Chapter 9

SPIRITECH! High Speed, High Def Christianity

You can't hasten the day or accelerate your destiny with the same old spiritual methods and tools. I want to furnish your Christianity with some brand new, updated, top of the line equipment that will do your job quicker and easier.

Unless you change your methods and tools, your zeal will only make you work longer and harder. That's not the *rest* that God is calling you into.

There is nothing wrong with the old equipment. It's just that the new is always better and more powerful. A hoe is an effective tool that can accomplish things, but a tiller is better. A typewriter can put the word on paper, but a computer & printer is better.

If you don't keep up with the times, you find that you will work harder than necessary while accomplishing less. That's why we must be willing to throw away some good old methods and tools, and trade them for some new things that we may not be experienced with.

People often resist new things because they are so familiar with the old. I remember my grandpa saying he hated air conditioning. People wouldn't have a telephone in their house, just because "they didn't like telephones". To some, cell phones are just a nuisance. Computers are unnecessary and complicated.

Let us not be that way where things of the Spirit are concerned!

The revelation of NOW has given me a wonderful way of receiving from God. I can remember how hard it once was to get *anything*! I fasted often. I did spiritual warfare against the devil. He always seemed to be successfully keeping my blessings from me. I would try to "birth" things, literally holding my belly as I groaned in a loud voice. I was always praying for breakthrough, and every inch of success came hard.

I must say that I did get some results with these methods, and that was actually what kept me trapped in them for so long. The little success I did find made me think I was doing things the right way. You can plow a field with a stick and a rock, but there might be a better way.

The methods I used are the tools of one who was warring from a position of lack. It was the position of one who was trying to get something that belongs to him, but for some reason I had to work for it.

I became very proficient at these old methods. I had much experience with them, and in my pursuit of the knowledge of these skills I was very acquainted with all of the biblical references to them. I grew to be very good at teaching them, and very good at inspiring others to be more zealous of these ways. If I was invited to speak, I was expected to expound on these "deeper things of God". It became a trademark of mine. It became my identity.

It takes a real humility to lose your life so you can really find His life.

When God began to bring me into the now zone, I found little use for my old tools. My main method would now be thanksgiving, because *thanksgiving* is a natural expression of someone who has *already* received something. Once I became convinced of the NOW, things happened quickly. It seemed all I did was acknowledge God's blessings, and they just came to me!

"And it shall come to pass, that before they call, I will answer; and while they are yet speaking, I will hear." – Isaiah 65:24

We Were Created For High Speed!

We need to understand that in the natural earth realm, God has accelerated things by revealing to mankind new ways of doing things. In the spiritual realm it is the same. The natural is a parallel of the spiritual.

There is a particular sect of Christianity that lives, works, and even dresses totally out of time. They will not use motorized equipment. Their clothes are from the American style of 100 years ago. They don't discern this time we are in, so they live totally out of it.

Let us not be guilty of living behind the times spiritually.

"Ye hypocrites, ye can discern the face of the sky and of the earth; but how is it that ye do not discern this time?" – Luke 12:56

We are a generation that was created to live in the now zone. We have come to expect things quickly. We like HIGH SPEED internet, INSTANT messaging, FAST food, IMMEDIATE credit approval, ONE HOUR photo, EXPRESS checkout, and EXPRESS mail. We are a DRIVE THROUGH, MICROWAVE kind of people. We have been conditioned for quick results.

We are different!

In the book of Ezra the people began rebuilding the temple of the Lord. In chapter three the foundation was laid and the young people begin to shout, sing and rejoice. When the old men came to see it they began to weep because the foundation was not as big as the former one, and this new temple would not be as great as the one before.

The sounds of joy and weeping were both so loud that the noise could not be discerned by those who were afar off.

(This is happening today. Some are excited about new things, while others seek former glories and see inferiority in this generation.)

The confusion brought discouragement, dissatisfaction, and finally disinterest, so the work on the temple stopped for many years.

(There must be a clear sound, a certain sound from Heaven if the church is to truly move forward. This NOW generation still has so many questions. They are looking for clarity. My hope is that this book can be a trumpet sound that pierces the junk, and gives you license and permission to live in the now zone.)

Then the Lord sent Haggai the prophet to pierce the confusion.

"...This people says, The time has not come, the time that the Lord's house should be built," – Hag.1:2

They had assumed that it wasn't God's timing for the finished work, so they lived on without it. They were living lives in which they sowed much but brought in little. They ate and were not full. They drank and were still thirsty. They were clothed, but still cold; and they earned money that disappeared (Hag. 1:6).

They thought they were in God's timing. They thought the abundant life must be for a later time instead of NOW.

But God said, *"Consider your ways"* (v. 7).

God's timing did not have them living that way. It was their own *ways* that had them living on a low level! God sent Haggai to change their ways. They needed to have their belief system corrected as well as their expectation.

The Lord then told them that this new temple was nothing compared to the old. He acknowledged its inferiority, but He made a statement that blew away any concern for the condition of the new temple.

"The glory of this latter temple shall be greater than the former..." – Hag. 1:9.

Hallelujah! He didn't say that the *house* would be greater. He said that the *glory* would be greater!

The voice of the old says that this generation should pray as in the former days, when they would pray all night until the sun came up. They speak of all night church services when they didn't care if they ever got home. They speak of the glory of former outpourings, and lament that the new church doesn't want to "pay the price" for such things.

I am now going to admit to you how inglorious I am. I like short and powerful and to the point church services. I don't like long ones. I get tired if you sing too many songs. I lose concentration if you preach too long. I loathe the idea of praying for something all night long. I want to pray it, say it, and get the answer. I don't want to pay the price. I've tried it, and I just can't do it. I'm too weak.

The former house can out-pray me, out-wait me, out-weep me, and out-preach me. I was built for speed. I was brought to the kingdom for such a time as this. I was not born out of time! I am perfectly equipped to walk in God's now zone! I am about receiving quickly from God, and then on to receiving something else. I am not built to spend my life waiting on something that is already mine.

Yes, I am a microwave Christian wanting drive through service. My calling is too big for me to sit around wishing and waiting. My anointing is for receiving. That's what I do.

I'm talking about this generation. Stop trying to be as glorious as the former house, and rejoice in the fact that God fills this latter, inferior house with *greater glory*!

"...He that glorieth, let him glory in the Lord." – I Cor. 1:31

Chapter 10

Reaping Where You Have Not Sown

"I sent you to reap that whereon ye bestowed no labor..." –
John 4:38

Don't you just love Jesus! Look at the above verse. He
really did "make all things new". Now you can receive based

solely on the goodness of God. You can be "rewarded" for doing absolutely nothing. This is good. I think it is called grace, unmerited favor!

"Say not ye, There are yet four months, and then cometh harvest? behold, I say unto you, Lift up your eyes, and look on the fields; for they are white already to harvest." – John 4:35

Jesus told us NOT to say that the harvest is four months away. He said to lift up our eyes, because the harvest is NOW!

I have lifted up my eyes. I see fullness and harvest. I can't help it. Once your eyes are open, you live with the wonderful open vision of God, who gives all things FREELY.

There is no way I could ever go back to the pattern of wishing… and hoping… and waiting… and praying. The open revelation will automatically make you a master receiver!

"…when the LORD thy God shall have brought thee into the land to give thee great and goodly cities, which thou buildedst not, And houses full of all good things, which thou filledst not, and wells digged, which thou diggedst not, vineyards and olive trees, which thou plantedst not…" – Deut. 6:10-11

The above verse gives us a picture of a NEW way to walk with God. In the NOW ZONE, all things are ready because of what the Lord has already done. If it's done, then any time is a good time for harvest!

"And he that reapeth receiveth wages, and gathereth fruit unto life eternal..." – John 4:36

We *reap*. We *receive*. We *gather*. This is our anointing, calling and purpose. The revelation of NOW anoints us this way, thereby creating a people who walk in the glory of God that can be seen by all flesh.

"And herein is that saying true, One soweth, and another reapeth. I sent you to reap that whereon ye bestowed no labour..." – John 4:37-38

The Father has done the work. He has prepared all things for harvest. That's why Jesus told us not to wait. It's ready for you!

I have a question for you. Is God that good? Is He good enough, and does He love us enough that He has provided all of the work necessary for us to walk on Earth as it is in Heaven?

Is He so good that He has provided for us a free gift of *zoe* life (life as God has it)?

Is our salvation that great? Are we complete in Him? Is this the rest we are to enter into?

Why is it that so many who talk of the *free gift* of God find it hard to attain such blessing?

It's because they don't have a NOW mindset. They are still trying to plow, sow, cultivate and toil for harvest. I have good news! We are called to reap where we've not sown!

The NOW believer simply acknowledges the blessing. When you really know that you are blessed *now*, you are like a magnet for heavenly manifestations. I love this life!

The blessings come upon you and overtake you. Goodness and mercy follow you all the days of your life. This is the will of God.

Things have been hard, and they have taken a long time because of our lack of knowledge. Let us leave the unfinished work, and move into the finished work.

I can no longer send people on a quest. I will never again make someone think they haven't prayed enough, fasted enough, labored enough, or waited enough. Your job is to *receive*. That's the only work left undone.

Aren't you glad that Jesus didn't think He had to do the work of John the Baptist again? Jesus didn't try to redo the work of one of the other prophets. He was in his own time! He was different from anything that had come before! So are you!

I can remember when I wanted to be like John the Baptist. I tried preaching like he did. I thought I saw a need for a ministry like his. Another time, I was Jeremiah the prophet. I wept and lamented our lowly condition.

I realize now that I was thousands of years too late for those ministries. They had already been done. I was living out of my time. I was living in the past.

It's time that we all catch up to speed. Jesus has come and paid all that needs to be paid. Not another drop of blood needs to be shed. Nobody has to die on the cross again. There is no more sacrifice for sin. We are the recipients of that awesome labor of Christ's death, burial, and resurrection! He finished the labor. We now receive!

"...He said, It is finished: and he bowed his head, and gave up the ghost." – John 19:30

"He said to me: **'It is done**. *I am the Alpha and the Omega, the Beginning and the End. To him who is thirsty I will give to drink without cost from the spring of the water of life.'"* – Rev. 21:6 NIV

"He shall see of the travail of his soul, and shall be satisfied: by his **knowledge** *shall my righteous servant justify many; for he shall bear their iniquities."* – Isaiah 53:11

It's because we *know* that we are in the reaping time that we can bypass all of the other waiting and labor. God has done so much for us, and it's His good pleasure to *give* us the kingdom! (Luke 12:32).

But what about the sovereign will of God? Doesn't the Bible say there is a time and season for everything and every purpose? Do we *move* with God's timing, or do we *determine* God's timing?

Many people think that Ecclesiastes 3 is telling us that it's *not* always reaping season. I will show you that it says just the opposite.

Read on...

Chapter 11

Eternity is in Your Heart

"To everything there is a season, and a time to every purpose under the heaven:" – Ecclesiastes 3:1

This chapter of Ecclesiastes goes on to list both good and bad things, saying there is a time for each. This passage of scripture is most often quoted when bad things are happening. To most of us, this explains that it's God's time for such things to occur, and there's nothing we can do about it.

First, let me teach you how to tell time in the Spirit. We are to know God's time by the *Spirit,* not outward circumstances!

"For as many as are led by the Spirit of God, they are the sons of God." – Romans 8:14

"...Oh ye hypocrites, ye can determine the face of the sky; but can ye not discern the signs of the times?" – Matt. 16:3

Any time God has told me to do something, the outward circumstances were never ready. If I waited for things around me to line up, I would never do *anything* for the Lord. I have obeyed Him in the face of circumstances that looked unchangeable. When I did, the outward manifestations would begin to bow to the vision God had put within me.

When I said I was going to go to Florida to start a church, everything went wrong. So many obstacles were popping up it was looking disastrous for us even before we left! Christians who loved me felt compelled to explain to us that God was trying to tell us through all of these "signs" that we weren't supposed to go.

Thank the Lord that I had already been taught not to be moved by circumstances, but only by the Word of God. I had heard the Word, and I was going. Sons of God are led by the Spirit, not outward circumstances. The bad things that were happening had absolutely nothing to say to me. I didn't need a sign. I had a word!

As I held to the Word of the Lord, the situation began to change and conform to the *correct* time of God.

We don't tell the time by circumstances because circumstances are usually *out of God's timing*! Only the Spirit knows the truth about what time it is.

Here's the conflict we live with: Within our spirit is a word of complete restoration, perfection, holiness, etc. Everything around us is contrary to that, so something has to bow and change; and it *won't* be the Word of God bowing and changing!

The circumstances have to change! But if you don't know that it's time for them to change, your life will continue to conform to the world around you.

I want this book to help you to have a conviction of the NOW time of God.

"He has made everything beautiful in its time. He has also set eternity in the hearts of men; yet they cannot fathom what God has done from beginning to end." – Ecclesiastes 3:11 NIV

"Eternity" is the Hebrew word "olam", which means "all time". There is a time for everything, but God has put *all*

time in our hearts. And though He has put eternity in our heart, this verse goes on to lament that nobody knows the works of God.

You have all the times of God in you! He doesn't want us to be ignorant of His works. In fact He is revealing His *finished* work to us! So the times of reaping are always within us. Times and seasons do not have to be something that comes to us from the outside circumstances of this fallen world. Let us not conform to this world! Let the world conform to the time of restoration and fullness that God has put *within* us.

People are waiting for the day when God's kingdom will be established. They think they are to wait and suffer until God makes everything around them wonderful.

*"One day the Pharisees asked Jesus, "When will the Kingdom of God come?" Jesus replied, "The Kingdom of God **can't be detected by visible signs**. You won't be able to say, 'Here it is!' or 'It's over there!' For the Kingdom of God is already among you."* – Luke 17:20-21 NLT

The kingdom comes from the inside out. My car came from the inside out. My world is changed from the inside out. Times are changed from the inside out!

The outward circumstances have yet to conform to the kingdom of God that is within us. One reason is because of what I quoted in Ecclesiastes 3:11. We have not fathomed what God has done from beginning to end.

"I know that whatever God does, it shall be forever. Nothing can be added to it..." – Ecclesiastes 3:14 NKJV

Nothing can be added to it because it's a finished work! Nothing *needs* to be added to it. It is complete!

When we are more *future* minded than *now* minded, we want God to do something that He hasn't done yet. We often pray in a way that is asking God to *add* something to our life.

God wants you to know that you have it all NOW. Nothing can be added to it. This is the way, walk ye in it.

"That which is has already been, and what is to be has already been; and God requires an account of what is past." – Ecclesiastes 3:15 NKJV

What you want, you already have, NOW! Whatever benefits you receive in the future, they were available the whole time!

Our prayers should be a gratitude for abundance, a thanksgiving for having all we will ever need. It has been done in Christ! God requires an account of what is already done. If it's been done, what are we waiting for? Are we waiting for God to add to His work?

Lose the wait! Our salvation is the NOW ZONE that holy men and prophets of old spoke of.

You have the secrets of God within you. The ways of the kingdom of Heaven are there. The promises are carried inside you. The fullness of time is there. Let us bring these things into outer manifestation. The world around you is conforming to the world within you.

God wants these things to come out of the secret place and into the outer court. That's why His Word is changing your mindset *from a cherub to a seraph...*

Chapter 12

When Cherubs Become Seraphs

"...Is a candle brought to be put under a bushel, or under a bed? and not to be set on a candlestick? For there is nothing hid, which shall not be manifested; neither was anything kept secret, but that it should come abroad." – Mark 4:21-22

This passage of scripture used to scare me. I thought it was a promise that all of my ugly secrets were going to be made know to everyone. I was so sin conscious and negative minded that I couldn't see what the Lord was saying here.

But I later realized that He wasn't speaking of anything ugly, or sinful, or dark. There was no mention of anything negative in the passage. Jesus was talking about the light! He was promising that the glory of God would not be kept secret. The lamp was not given to us just so we could talk about something that nobody could see. He promised that it would be seen outwardly!

There is a place called the holy of holies, beyond the veil, the third day, the promised land, in the Spirit, the secret place of the Most High. It's in that place where you hear and perceive the mysteries, or secrets of God. These are things that only He knows, until He shows it to you.

"The secret things belong unto the LORD our God: **but those things which are revealed belong unto us** *and to our children for ever..."* – Deut. 29:29.

The secret is then carried within you. You may call it a promise, a vision, or a sense of destiny. Oftentimes it seems that it may never happen, but whenever you go back to that secret place, you hear the same Word again for it never changes. You are encouraged, rejuvenated, and empowered to continue by what you see and hear beyond the veil.

With the revelation (or unveiling) of NOW, God is taking things out of the secret place and into the outer court. In other words, things like healing will not just be a promise, but an outward manifestation! The fullness of God will not be a prophecy, but a lifestyle!

I have found that most of God's people praise Him more for the *promises* than for what is actually happening in their lives. They might have a mess all around them, but they have found a place of refuge in the Spirit. They have learned to "enter in". They have learned to come into that place by prayer, praise, and worship.

This is good, but too often it is a temporary visitation into the most holy place. We have become so good and experienced at "entering in" to that place because we always leave it. We then become slimed or battered by the world's conditions and we have to find that feel good place of promise again.

But what if our life was exactly like the promises and the glory we see when we are in the secret place? What if you never had to "enter in" again? What if the Word of God was not just something you knew, but was something that those around you could see?

Do you know what? The only thing that has to happen is for the veil to rip open. Then whatever glory was confined beyond the veil will flood out into the outer court!

"Then the glory of the LORD went up from the cherub, and stood over the threshold of the house; and the house was filled with the cloud, and the court was full of the brightness of the LORD's glory." – Ezekiel 10:4

Ezekiel saw the glory of God coming out of the secret place, filling the outer court. The veil that keeps the glory confined is done away in Christ, but can still cover your eyes. That's why you need a *revelation*, or *revealing*, or an *unveiling*. When you have that, the glory comes out into your outer body and outer circumstances! All you need is the truth. Truth reveals the glory. The Word of God is the sword that pierces and rips the veil.

If you see the temple of God correctly, you don't see a sanctuary divided from the holy of holies. It has been renovated! The veil of partition is removed in Christ, and the glory comes out!

You don't have to "enter in" to the glory beyond the veil. If you have a revelation (unveiling), the glory comes out. It arises upon you. It will not be a secret in the secret place. All flesh will see it! (Isaiah 60) The Glory of the LORD HAS Risen upon you,

The veil is your flesh, your carnal mindset (Hebrews 10:20). It hinders your ability to see the NOW. It also keeps others from seeing the glory that you carry within.

Cherubs

Notice that Ezekiel said he saw the glory of God going up from the cherub. Cherubs are anointed (or equipped and empowered) to *cover* the glory (Ezekiel 28:14). Cherubs *cover* the Lord on the mercy seat. Cherubs are embroidered into the veil that *confines* the glory to the secret place. Not only that, but when Solomon built the temple, he put wall to wall Cherubs in front of the veil, as if they were standing at sentry, making sure none can pass through.

"...you shut up the kingdom of Heaven... for you neither go in yourselves, nor do you allow those who are entering to go in."
– Matt. 23:13

We are the cherubs! We are experts at covering God's glory. We cover it without even trying. That's how good we are. Our empowering equipment is our carnal mindset.

We don't *want* to be cherubs, but we are. We want to *release* the glory of God. We want it to be *seen*. That's why we are always praying for God to manifest. The cry of our heart is that He would be seen among us. We want Him to be heard, felt, and revealed to all!

We indict ourselves as a cherub with this cry. We know that God abides within us, but He is hidden. We know that His glory is in us, but we pray earnestly for it to be manifest. We know He is covered up inside us, but we don't know how to release it so we pray more. We pray longer. We pray louder.

We know it is our own flesh that covers the Lord. We pray that others would not see us, but see Him. We pray that they would not just hear us, but hear Him. We know the Lord is in us, and we know we are keeping Him covered. We are cherubs.

Remember, Ezekiel saw the Lord's glory *coming out* from the cherubs. They would not be able to cover Him forever!

Remember also, that Jesus said there is nothing in secret that shall not be manifested. The secret that was hid from the ages (Christ in you, the hope of glory) will not remain a secret. The world around you will see it!

God is giving the cherubs a new sound. This sound is transforming them, renewing their mind. They are seeing and saying things differently. The sound is equipping them to release God's glory. Like Gideon's army, the earthen vessels that covered the torches are broken when they hear the trumpet sound!

The sound is changing them. Those who once effortlessly *covered* the glory are becoming those who effortlessly *release* the glory.

"And as we have borne the image of the earthy, we shall also bear the image of the heavenly." - I Cor. 15:49

You weren't born again just so you could live your life covering God's glory. You were not called to live all of your days as a cherub. You were destined to live as a *seraph.*

Seraphs

Isaiah, chapter six, describes the Lord sitting on His throne, or mercy seat; and the train of His robe filled the temple (spilling out into the whole house).

But instead of cherubs covering the Lord, Isaiah calls them seraphs. The description of their appearance is similar to the cherubs, but with a major difference.

These guys are on fire!

The word "seraph" means: *a fiery being,* or a *flaming one.*

These guys aren't *covering* the glory. They are *releasing* the glory and it's seen upon them!

"For our God is a consuming fire." – Hebrews 12: 29

Not only do they *look* different. They *sound* different!

"And one cried to another and said: 'Holy, holy, holy is the Lord of Hosts. The whole earth is full of His glory!'" – Isaiah 6:3

Do you see the NOW in their language? Other references to the glory filling the earth were spoken as a prophecy or promise. Before, it was spoken that the earth *will be* filled with God's glory.

These seraphs are saying the earth *is filled* with His glory! They see it! To them this is not a future event. It's a NOW reality! If you can see the NOW glory, you will find it manifesting.

The truth is, God poured His Spirit into the earth on the Day of Pentecost. It's here! All you need now is the *knowledge* of His glory.

*"For the earth shall be filled with the **knowledge** of the glory of the LORD, as the waters cover the sea."* – Habakkuk 2:14

Habakkuk said we would know it. We would know it in a way that goes beyond wanting it and waiting for it.

In The Revelation of Jesus Christ, John also saw these "living beings" in and around the throne. Here's how he described them:

*"Each of the four living creatures had six wings and were covered with eyes, **inside and out**."* – Rev. 4:8 GWT

This means they not only could see on the inside, but they also saw on the outside. The promises of God are not just an inward knowing. They are also an outward happening! God has equipped us with the *knowledge* of His glory that brings the reality of the kingdom of God out of the secret place, and into the outer court!

God has spoken that the inner will be seen on the outer. Expect it! Let it become your identity. Be transformed by the renewing of your mind. Become a NOW son of God!

If you will turn to look at this NOW Word of God, the veil will be removed and you will be changed into what you see. You don't have to try to make it happen. Just be willing to look at it.

You will never be the same.

Read on...

Chapter 13

NOW Vision

"And the vision of all is become unto you as the words of a book that is sealed, which men deliver to one that is learned, saying, Read this, I pray thee: and he saith, I cannot; for it is sealed." – Isaiah 29:11

This passage in Isaiah describes the condition of God's people in that day. The prophets and seers weren't seeing, so nobody else could see with clear spiritual vision. In fact, the Lord said that their ability to see was like a sealed book; the word was a secret mystery, and nobody could see it.

He also described their hypocrisy. Their words and their lives weren't matching up (v. 13).

Most of us have this type of hypocrisy to some degree. Even the most sincere believers who are passionately pursuing God can have it. They speak the promises of God, yet they are still waiting for the promises to come into manifestation. Their words and actual lifestyle are not matching up.

God wants to bridge this gap between what you are professing and what you are experiencing. He does want fullness for you NOW. He wants to rid us of this hypocrisy so that our words and our experience are the same!

So how does the Lord fix this hypocrisy? Will He send us a minister, who will stir us to try harder? Will He bring a movement of "holiness" that will shame us into getting it right? Will He shame us to the point of desperation, so we will finally pay the price to get the power?

NO! God has promised to do *"a marvelous work and a wonder"* (v. 14). He said that the day would come when the blind would see and the deaf would hear the words of the book. The vision would not be *sealed*, but *revealed*! This is how He would fix it. The Lord would simply open our eyes. We would see, and when we see with this open revelation, our lives would become like our words!

"And in that day shall the deaf hear the words of the book, and the eyes of the blind shall see out of obscurity, and out of darkness. The meek also shall increase their joy in the LORD, and the poor among men shall rejoice in the Holy One of Israel." – Isaiah 29:18-19

"They also that erred in spirit shall come to understanding..." – Isaiah 29:24.

The apostle John saw in a vision, the revelation of Jesus Christ. He stands in the presence of God and His throne. There is a crystal sea. There are living beings "both in and around the throne". (We are in Him, and He is in us). There is a river of life, a tree of life, and there is no more curse. All that mankind has needed and desired is in Him.

But in Revelation chapter five, John sees a book in the hand of God. The book is sealed, and nobody was able to open the book or to look at it. John broke down and cried because nobody could open that book.

I know why he wept. The cry of every man's heart is met in Christ. Healing is in the tree of life. There is a river of life. Anyone can drink of it and never thirst again. All things are restored, yet nobody could see it. The book (vision, ability to see) was sealed.

There is a river, yet people thirst. There is a tree whose leaves heal, yet people are sick. The glory is here, yet people grope blindly for it. Everything that everyone needs is right in front of their noses, yet they do without it because they can't see it.

In Genesis 29, a woman named Hagar and her son were dying of thirst in the desert:

*"And God opened her eyes, and she **saw** a well of water; and she went, and filled the bottle with water, and gave the lad drink."* – Genesis 21:19

God did not have to create a well for her to drink from. It was there all the time! The woman nearly died of thirst with a well of water right in front of her!

This is why my heart goes out to my brothers and sisters in the Lord. I see so many thirsty, hungry, needy souls who love the Lord so much. They struggle and do without, because they are unable to see what has been set before them. Because they can't see it, they keep asking God to give it to them. They just don't know that they don't have to wait. They can have it NOW if they can see it.

John is crying in Revelation chapter five for this same reason, but then he is told not to cry anymore; for Jesus has prevailed to break the seals (veil) and to open the book (vision, ability to see the glory).

The Lamb of God then took the book out of the hand of Him who sat on the throne. (The secret things that once belonged only to the Father are now revealed to the sons of men through Christ!)

When He took the book, the living beings that were both in and around the throne (us) began to sing a new song:

*"And they sung a new song, saying, Thou art worthy to take the book, and to open the seals thereof: for thou wast slain, and hast redeemed us to God by thy blood out of every kindred, and tongue, and people, and nation; And hast made us unto our God kings and priests: and **we shall reign on the earth**."* – Revelation 5:9-10

The ability to see brings a *new song*! They left their old song behind and embraced a new sound. The new sound was a sound of redemption. It was a sound declaring what is seen in the open revelation of Christ. We are kings. We are priests, and we shall reign on the earth!

When shall we reign? On the earth! In other words, NOW! We aren't waiting for the afterlife or another dispensation, or even another week. We throw away that old song. This isn't the same old song and dance. This is a sound of NOW. The seals are broken. The book is open.

NOW we see! NOW we know! NOW we are. We drink from the river NOW. We do not thirst and we don't have to do without. When the Lord opened our eyes, *we lost the wait.*

When people ask me how they can pray for me, I tell them to just pray that I can see more. If I see more, I will simply walk in more of the fullness of God.

There are specific things that I am still expecting to happen in my life, but I don't tell people to ask God to give them to me. Nothing can be added to what He has already done. Let us pray than we can simply see what is in front of us NOW.

"That the God of our Lord Jesus Christ, the Father of glory, may give unto you the spirit of wisdom and revelation in the knowledge of him: The eyes of your understanding being enlightened..." – Ephesians 1:17-18.

When your eyes are opened, it's like coming out of a hypnotic trance. You wake up spiritually. You are energized. You feel your dominion. You actually break free from an enemy who had you hypnotized.

The enemy's name is: *"Later"*.

Read on…

Chapter 14

The Hypnotic Seduction of "*Later*"

"Later" is a mindset that has been drilled into Christianity for ages. For many, *everything* is later. To them, there is just not much good to be expected until after you die. Then you will be happy. Then you won't be sick. Then we will get a big house. Then we will be rich (our streets will paved with gold).

When I first got saved, nearly all of the songs we would sing in church were about dying and going to Heaven, or flying and going to Heaven. It was all about how happy we would be, how we would then sing and shout the victory, how we wouldn't be sick anymore.

We sang about leaving this old world of pain and sorrow, this place of trial and affliction. To us, *now* was bad. *Later* would be good.

We read our Bibles and saw all of the wonderful benefits and blessings of new life in Jesus, but we pushed them all into the afterlife. We simply could not fathom a life on earth with such blessing and joy. Our carnal minds could not receive the things of God in the NOW, so we placed them all into another time.

"But the natural man receiveth not the things of the Spirit of God: for they are foolishness unto him: neither can he know them, because they are spiritually discerned." – I Cor. 2:14

The only way we could acknowledge such a wonderful life was to accept it in the most remote form available, the afterlife.

This was the Christianity I was born into. I was fine with it and sang as loud as the rest of them. I had no promise of this life, nor was I looking for it. I just wanted to make sure I made it to Heaven.

But God wouldn't let me stop there. He began showing me that the promises were for *this* life. I embraced that idea, but my thought patterns were still stuck in "*later*" mode.

I began believing in healing, abundance, and restoration in this life, but I struggled to experience it in my own condition. For many years I confessed these benefits. I preached them to others, but I seemed to be chasing them more than living in them.

I was still gripped by the power of a stronghold in my mind. It hindered my ability to receive with a subtle little poison in my thought patterns. It was mixed into my faith in God's promises, and it short circuited my life. It was a little deceptive enemy called "*later*".

Later holds the promises of God right out in front of you like a carrot on a string. It never says NOW. It's always later. It keeps you in preparation for later. All of your days seem like a preliminary for the real thing, later.

STOP LIVING FOR *LATER*! You don't have to be just a possibility. NOW are we the sons of God. Don't be mesmerized by a promise that stays just a day out of reach. Live in the present!

To break the power of *later*, you must rebel against it. Today you live! Today you experience Heaven on Earth! Take on your NOW identity. You are blessed NOW. You have it all NOW. Today is a good day. God is here today!

Don't wait for God to bless you. Be blessed! Take on the identity of someone who lives Heavenly life today!

Don't worry about outward manifestations. Just know who you are! The outward manifestations will bow and change and conform to who you are in your mentality.

"As a man thinketh in his heart, so is he." – Proverbs 23:7

We have been conditioned to expect everything later, but fresh vision is changing our expectation. When we wake up, we know the heavens are open. We are not waiting. We are walking in goodness and mercy *all* the days of our life.

This is it! Look out world. We are here! Creation, you can quit your groaning because we have NOW come into our own!

We are not on some upward climb. We stand atop Mount Zion, NOW. We're not breaking through the veil. God's glory is all over us, NOW.

I will never need another breakthrough as long as I live. Jesus broke through for me and I benefit NOW. I will never again try to climb the holy mountain. I've been elevated by Him. The Lord is my shepherd. I SHALL NOT WANT!

I have written this book because I have seen the results of the revelation of NOW. It has changed everything for me. I love God more than ever before. I can now commune with Him on a level that I never dreamed possible. I enjoy Him, and I enjoy my salvation. I enjoy life for it is truly an *abundant* life!

It was after I saw the revelation of NOW that I became truly satisfied with God's goodness. I have noticed my love for people overwhelms me and gives me such a supernatural peace. Those who know me also know that my life is drama free.

I haven't had a, flu, or headache since 1982, and I cannot conceive the idea of ever being sick again.

My marriage, my children, my ministry – blessed!

I'm not waiting to die. I'm not waiting for another dispensation. I'm not waiting for another outpouring. In God I live and move and have my very being, NOW.

When the Word of God has removed every reason that you have to wait, you become one who is lives in the NOW ZONE. The Lord is truly removing the tares from the wheat. When He does, you will shine like the sun in the kingdom of your Father (Matt. 13:43).

Do you have any questions? Of course you do. I will address some common ones in the next chapter...

Chapter 15

Questions

What about patience?

Don't we have to wait on some things in order to learn patience?

What is the difference between "NOW people" and impatient people?

In the past, there would be times when I would feel frustrated by waiting. I decided that God must have been testing my patience, so I focused on passing the test and having a good attitude while I waited.

But it seemed that my patience was *always* being tried. I waited long for everything. I was fine with it. I was so fine with it that I was an expert at waiting for later and doing without.

After so many years, who wanted to know if I could wait? God knew. I knew. In fact, I expected to wait. Why was I always being tested in the area of patience? What kind of teacher gives a student the same test over and over, especially when the student passes the test?

I will admit that I didn't always like it. It wasn't always easy, and I would feel frustration at times; but I would comfort myself with "patience and promise" scriptures, and I would exercise patience.

I must also admit that I very rarely feel that frustration anymore! The NOW ZONE has changed me!

Biblical patience is a fruit of the Spirit, a natural manifestation of His life. It is *not* a skill that we learn through repetition. Like all fruit of the Spirit there is a natural man's counterfeit. We produce the counterfeit by trying to develop the real by our efforts.

For years I tried to produce more love, joy, peace, etc. My efforts have now ceased. I'm not building spiritual muscles anymore. My fruit has been produced, not by my efforts, not by much trial, but by the gracious, Spirit of God who gives us all things *freely*.

When I saw that God is withholding no good thing from me, when I realized I have everything NOW, my frustration left. God is not telling me to wait, so I am not frustrated in the flux of wondering when I will get it. Patience is automatic. I have such peace because I know things are happening even as I write this.

I have a sense of fullness and completeness in God. The questions of "Will God do it?" or "*When* will God do it" are virtually nonexistent in my life. The revelation of NOW has put me right where I need to be to receive the promises of God.

I didn't arrive at this place of patience by passing a million tests. Patience became a natural fruit in my life when I entered the NOW ZONE. It wasn't a long process that got me there. It was a revelation. I feel complete and satisfied.

"*...my people shall be satisfied with my goodness, saith the LORD.*" – Jeremiah 31:14

I'm not waiting on God so there is no frustration. I'm not even waiting on myself, because I'm looking into this NOW Word. I'm growing and the things of God are manifesting more and more. Even if it still takes a little time to receive some things, I don't feel like I'm waiting. Patience is automatic.

Because of what I now see. I am patient with others. I am patient with the body of Christ (I was totally not like this before). I am patient with myself.

The NOW ZONE will help you skip the fleshly "process". You can go to the head of the line and walk in the fruit of the Spirit NOW.

"But many that are first shall be last; and the last shall be first." – Matthew 19:30

Doesn't it take a growth process to get us to the NOW ZONE?

No! Be careful of the word *"process"*! Most people who adhere to a *process* Christianity die in the *process*. Every bad thing that happens to them is part of the *process*. They never get out of the *process*, and finally they are literally *processed* to death.

One eye opening revelation from God can do more for you than seven years of bad luck.

I believed for years that I was being processed, but the process brought little, if any **progress**.

"Ever learning, and never able to come to the knowledge of the truth." – II Timothy 3:7

Revelation is supernatural. Process is natural. Every religion uses a process because they are not based on the finished work of Christ.

If you are looking for methods of improvement in this book, you won't find any. I can only tell you about the NOW ZONE. There has to be a supernatural unveiling of these things. If you are seeing it you know it, and if you *know* it things will change!

We grow by revelation, which means revealing or uncovering. God is uncovering what has been there all the time.

If there is any process, it is really just growth in the knowledge of God. Real growth comes from seeing the finished work of Christ.

Aren't there instances where the timing is actually better if it comes later instead of now?

I don't claim to know everything, so I will just say that we have used the excuse of God's timing more than we should.

Timing comes into play more if we are talking about direction from God, such as having a conversation with someone. Some times are better than others. God may tell me to start a church in Africa, but maybe not tomorrow. Timing can be involved.

Generally, if we are talking about a promise or benefit that is in our covenant with God, a benefit that has been provided and paid for; NOW is the acceptable time of wholeness and deliverance.

People think that God will delay the answered prayer to teach them something in the time of waiting. He can teach you something today! He's that good at it! Anything God can do next month, He can do NOW.

What about suffering in the flesh?

Aren't we called to suffer for the Lord?

Jesus came to end the suffering of mankind. Suffering was brought about by sin, which was taken care of at the cross. Suffering was a part of the curse, and Christ has redeemed us from that (Galatians 3:13).

Nearly every reference of suffering in the New Testament is dealing with persecution, ostracizing, and other acts of people because of our stand for the gospel of Jesus Christ. These references always encourage the Christians to understand it and endure it like we should. We are told to face it with love and faith.

The New Testament does not include things like *getting sick* in the category of suffering for Christ. Nowhere does it indicate that we are to partake of the curses of the fallen world. That would not make sense for God to redeem us from those things and then put them back on us. If the Lord wanted to use the curses to perfect us, He didn't have to give His Son. He would just torture us into perfection.

The only reference I know of in the New Testament that may be speaking of another suffering would be the verse that calls us to *"suffer in the flesh"* to cease from sin (I Pet. 4:1). The passage then continues to speak of denying the lusts.

This is the hardship of denying temptation, resisting sin, and saying "no" to carnal inclinations. It makes the flesh cry and throw a fit, but let it suffer.

Why does the Bible say we will be glorified AFTER we've suffered a while?

When you read the context of that statement, which is found in I Peter chapter five, you will find that it is talking about resisting sin *and* dealing with persecution for the gospel's sake.

Again, if we are talking about suffering natural affliction, sicknesses, curses, and just the bad things in life; if we must partake of these things before we can be glorified, I have a question for you:

What have we *been* doing?! We've suffered these things for thousands of years! How much more? How many more suicides? How many more nights of crying ourselves to sleep? How much more pain?

We have *been* suffering! NOW it's time for glorification!

Chapter 16

Will I Live in the Now Zone?

Life in the now zone is a natural product of truly believing in the NOW. We who believe in the NOW happen to know some things concerning this wonderful salvation we have!

1. We know that the Lord has done all of the labor for us. There is nothing left undone, except for the receiving of these things He has abundantly provided.

2. We know that God loves us. He likes us. He digs us. He's happy for us. It's His good pleasure to give us the kingdom. Now faith pleases Him, because when we have it we can finally receive from Him, NOW.

3. We know that our own weaknesses and imperfections have nothing to do with this. We have it all now anyway.

4. We know that God wants His will to be done, *"on earth as it is in Heaven"*. We expect life on earth to be good, like it is in Heaven.

5. We know that God is not holding out on us. The payment for abundant life was huge. It's time we receive.

6. We know that God does not tarry. He has provided before we ever knew how to receive it.

If these statements are in line with the way you think, look out! You are about to see some changes!

The great thing about faith is that it automatically produces. "As a man thinks, so is he". "According to your faith, be it unto you".

I have written this simply to help you to see something more clearly. I hope it has helped to kill some weak and beggarly elements in your belief.

Have some questions been answered? Did you feel your spirit leap within you as you read certain things in this book? Does it seem like you've really known these things all along in your spirit, but now it has stepped forth?

You don't have to be great, or strong, or deep, or super spiritual to walk in the NOW ZONE. All you have to do is see. If you see these things with a conviction you will never go back.

It's about to get real good! You are seeing things that the prophets of old were told about. They wanted to see what you see.

"But blessed are your eyes, for they see: and your ears, for they hear. For verily I say unto you, That many prophets and righteous men have desired to see those things which ye see, and have not seen them; and to hear those things which ye hear, and have not heard them." – Matthew 13:16-17

Get ready for some high speed Christianity! Get ready for acceleration! Dreams are becoming reality!

God has put you in the game. You are not on the sidelines waiting for the call. You can be who you always knew you were! You can be that today!

"Then the LORD replied: "Write down the revelation and make it plain on tablets so that a herald may run with it." – Habbakuk 2:2 NIV

Chapter 17

I'm Ready! What Now?

As I was writing chapter one of this book I paused, and smiled as I remembered how the Lord caused me to receive a car supernaturally. I felt pleased that I could use this testimony to teach and inspire others.

I was then interrupted by the voice of the Lord. I heard Him say, "Son, you still have that faith. You still live in the NOW ZONE."

Immediately, I became aware that there was a situation in my life in which I was neglecting the very truth that I was teaching.

We had put one of our houses up for sale. I remember sticking the "for sale" sign in the ground and rejoicing at the thought of the profit we would make. Teresa and I thanked God for a quick sale. We decreed that there was a perfect buyer, and the Lord would put it all together.

Thirty days had soon passed with no sale. We continued to speak the right things.

Now it was over sixty days when the Lord reminded me that I was still in the NOW ZONE. I simply had let it slip. I had reverted to cruise control. I had gone back into "eventual" faith. I was so busy with other things that this house deal had gone under the radar.

So there I was, Mr. NOW ZONE with a house I couldn't sell.

But when the Lord brought this situation to my attention, my spirit stirred up. I remembered where I live, the NOW ZONE. God wasn't tarrying, and I didn't have to wait.

Whoever was going to buy that house was out there somewhere, and my fast Heavenly Father wanted to put the deal together!

I told my wife what the Lord had told me. She said she heard the same thing that very evening.

We looked at each other with faith filled eyes and said, "Tomorrow, we are getting a call. We're not waiting anymore!"

You know what happened, right?

The next day we got the call and sold the house!

Thank God for the Spirit of truth. He leads, guides, and **reminds** us.

*"But the Counselor, the Holy Spirit, whom the Father will send in my name, will teach you all things and will **remind** you of everything I have said to you."* – John 14:26

So what do you do now?

You just have to remember *who* you are and *where* you are. You're a NOW son of God, and you live in the NOW ZONE!

Remember that as soon as you pray, angels are dispatched and activity is buzzing in the spirit. NOW faith makes your angels put their playing cards down and go to work for you!

Don't let your angels get bored!

"What are all the angels? They are spirits sent to serve those who are going to receive salvation." – Hebrews 1:14

Chapter 18

A Final Word

"Of His own will He brought us forth by the Word of truth, that we might be a kind of firstfruits of His creatures." – James 1:18

You were brought to the kingdom for such a time as this. You have probably been through much, but here you are ready for a new day.

You have a sense of destiny. You are to be a showcase of God's glory, and a trophy of His goodness.

You are hearing a certain sound from Heaven because The Lord is raising you up to be an example of things not seen before by man.

You are a kind of first fruit of the new creation. Creation has groaned, wanting to see someone like you. When creation sees you standing on the mountaintop, creation is soon to follow. You are a kind of first fruit.

You are an expression of how good it can be. You demonstrate fullness. You are a clear picture of the finished work of Christ.

You're not hungry for the glory of God. You wear it!

This is who you are. Remember your identity every day. This is not a day to shrink back so that others can't see your inadequacies. It's a day rise and shine like sons of God should!

What you have is the answer for the world's problems. While others align with political camps and philosophical ideology, you are a sign and a wonder. You are a demonstration of abundant life!

You have the green light from your Father. Go ahead! Live the life!

You can feel yourself shining from within as you embrace the NOW Word. This glory will attract good things. Favor, health, opportunities, people, and financial resources are attracted to you!

Welcome to the kingdom of light!

God has set things in order, so that the universe produces for you. When our vision becomes clear, we walk in earth as it is in Heaven.

Gone are the days of the earth giving forth grudgingly. There is no more famine (Ezekiel 34:29). We no longer eat by the sweat of our brow. The blessings come upon us and overtake us. Thorns and thistles are not to be expected in our garden. For the earth shall never again be cursed for our sake!

This is God's realm. This is the NOW ZONE. You go from glory to glory, from mountaintop to mountaintop, from faith to faith. This is your promised land. This is your inheritance.

"...your ears will hear a voice behind you, saying, "This is the way; walk in it." – Isaiah 30:21

This is the way. Learn it. Live it. Enjoy it!

Welcome home. Welcome to the NOW ZONE.

Chapter 19

NOW Scriptures!

The following references are biblical promises and statements that describe and declare the NOW ZONE.

"Son of man, what is this proverb you have in the land of Israel: 'The days go by and every vision comes to nothing'?
Say to them, 'This is what the Sovereign LORD says: I am going to put an end to this proverb, and they will no longer quote it in Israel.' Say to them, 'The days are near when every vision will be fulfilled...

But I the LORD will speak what I will, and it shall be fulfilled without delay. For in your days... I will fulfill whatever I say, declares the Sovereign LORD'...

Son of man, the house of Israel is saying, 'The vision he sees is for many years from now, and he prophesies about the distant future.'

Therefore say to them, 'This is what the Sovereign LORD says: None of my words will be delayed any longer; whatever I say will be fulfilled, declares the Sovereign LORD.'' – Ezekiel 12:22-28 NIV

"And it shall come to pass, that before they call, I will answer; and while they are yet speaking, I will hear." – Isaiah 65:24

"The time will come," says the LORD, "when the grain and grapes will grow faster than they can be harvested..." – Amos 9:13 NLT

And except those days should be shortened, there should no flesh be saved: but for the elect's sake those days shall be shortened." – Matthew 24:22

For he says, "At the right time I heard you, and on a day of salvation I helped you." Listen, now is really the "right time"! Now is the "day of salvation"! - II Corinthians 6:2 ISV

"So God set another time for entering his rest, and that time is today. God announced this through David much later in the

already quoted: "Today when you hear his voice, don't harden your hearts." – Hebrews 4:7 NLT

*"And sware by him that liveth for ever and ever, who created heaven, and the things that therein are, and the earth, and the things that therein are, and the sea, and the things which are therein, that **there should be time no longer:"** –* Revelation 10:6

About the Author

MINISTRY

Rick is a spirit-filled minister, motivator, and encourager. He is a mentor and advisor to many Christian leaders.. Countless lives have been transformed as he has preached and taught thousands of speaking engagements.

Using personal examples of faith adventures, self-effacing humor, and a clear lifestyle example, Rick leads and encourages people to experience the Kingdom of Heaven in this life. His message is that God has given us all we need in Jesus Christ, and if we believe, we can enjoy every bit of it.

Because, Rick has an ability to relate to all types of people, he is invited to many different kinds of groups, churches and organizations.

LIFESTYLE

A youthful, vibrant 50-something who hasn't had a flu or headache in over since 1982.

The Lord has blessed him with prosperity and success as a husband, minister, and businessman.

Rick and his wife Judi make their home in beautiful central Florida.

HISTORY, BACKGROUND & EXPERIENCE

Saved from a life of drugs, alcohol abuse and crime in 1979 at the age of 21.

Attended Rhema Bible Training Center in '83-'84.

Associate Pastor '84-'88.

Pastor '89-'98.

Itinerant Minister '98-present.

To contact Rick Manis Ministries
Please write or call.

PO Box 784327
Winter Garden FL 34778

918-277-3458

Or visit us on the web at:
Rickmanis.com

Or email us at:
rick@rickmanis.com

If you liked *"The Now Zone"* you will **love** these other books
by Rick Manis

FULLNESS! *Living Beyond Revivals & Outpourings*

&

Glory in the Glass

Order online at Rickmanis.com
Or call 918-277-3458

You may also be interested in:

"Heaven on Earth University"

This *Life Mastery Course* is an audio curriculum you can study at home at your own pace.

Learn to master the human experience with this interactive study system that deals with every area of life.

The curriculum includes:

- 18 Lessons
- 8 CD
- DVD
- Workbook
- Graduation Certificate

All for $50!

Order online at Rickmanis.com

Or call 918-277-3458

67016013R00081

Made in the USA
Lexington, KY
30 August 2017